Journey Through Space
The Moon

Reagan Miller

Crabtree Publishing Company

www.crabtreebooks.com

Author: Reagan Miller
Publishing plan research and development:
  Sean Charlebois, Reagan Miller
  Crabtree Publishing Company
Project development: Clarity Content Services
Project management: Clarity Content Services
Editors: Kristi Lindsay, Wendy Scavuzzo
Copy editor: Dimitra Chronopoulos
Proofreader: Kathy Middleton
Design: First Image
Cover design: Samara Parent
Photo research: Linda Tanaka
Production coordinator: Ken Wright
Prepress technician: Ken Wright
Print coordinator: Katherine Berti

Photographs:
NASA: pp 4, 5, 7 lower, 8, 13 left, 16, 20, 21; Matej
Pavlansky/shutterstock: p6; Luc Viatour/NASA: p9;
martiin fluidworkshop/shutterstock: p10; Catalin
Petolea/shutterstock: p11; Luc Viatour/NASA: p13;
David M. Schrader/shutterstock: p14; Molodec/
shutterstock, Rafael Pacheco/shutterstock: p15 top;
iStockphoto/Thinkstock, Manuel Castillo/European
Space Agency: p19 top; Larry Pieniazek/CCL/Wikipedia:
p21 lower; iStockphoto/Thinkstock: p22; D&D
Photos/shutterstock: Background photo; © Carmen
Martínez Banús/iStockphoto: front cover (girl); Media
Union/ shutterstock: front cover (city); Getideaka/
shutterstock: front cover (moon); Thinkstock: back cover

Library and Archives Canada Cataloguing in Publication

Miller, Reagan
  The moon / Reagan Miller.

(Journey through space)
Includes index.
Issued also in electronic format.
ISBN 978-0-7787-5306-3 (bound).--ISBN 978-0-7787-5311-7 (pbk.)

  1. Moon--Juvenile literature. I. Title. II. Series: Journey through
space (St. Catharines, Ont.)

QB582.M56 2012   j523.3   C2012-901242-4

Library of Congress Cataloging-in-Publication Data

CIP available at Library of Congress

Crabtree Publishing Company
www.crabtreebooks.com   1-800-387-7650

Printed in the U.S.A./032012/CJ20120215

Published in Canada
Crabtree Publishing
616 Welland Ave.
St. Catharines, Ontario
L2M 5V6

Published in the United States
Crabtree Publishing
PMB 59051
350 Fifth Avenue, 59th Floor
New York, New York 10118

Published in the United Kingdom
Crabtree Publishing
Maritime House
Basin Road North, Hove
BN41 1WR

Published in Australia
Crabtree Publishing
3 Charles Street
Coburg North
VIC 3058

3 5444 00114322 0

The Moon

What Is a Moon?

The word "moon" is used to describe an object that **orbits**, or travels around, a planet. Most planets have moons. Earth has only one moon. Other planets have many moons. Jupiter has 63 moons! Moons have different shapes, sizes, and colors.

Jupiter is a planet with a large red spot. Jupiter's moons vary in size and color.

Jupiter

Red Spot

Earth's moon is the fifth largest in the whole solar system. The solar system is made up of the Sun, planets, moons, and other objects in space.

Earth's Moon

The Moon is Earth's closest neighbor in space. It is about 238,855 miles (384,400 kilometers) from Earth. That might sound like a huge distance, but the Moon is much closer to Earth than any other object in space. Earth and the Moon are part of the solar system.

Both Earth and the Moon are **spheres**.

The Moon is the closest object to Earth in space.

On the Moon

Even though they are neighbors, the Moon and Earth are very different. There is no air or liquid water on the Moon. There is no life on the Moon. The temperature on the Moon becomes very hot during the day, then very cold during the night.

The Moon is much smaller than Earth.

The Moon's Surface

The Moon's surface is covered with **craters**, or holes. Scientists believe that the craters were caused by large rocks that crashed into the Moon. Some of the craters are very small. Some craters are huge. The Moon's largest crater is larger than Canada!

What Do You "Sea"?

The dark areas on the Moon are large **plains**. The plains were formed when lava from the Moon's center filled craters on the Moon's surface. Long ago, people thought that these dark areas were seas. These places are called *maria*, which is the Latin word for seas.

Have you ever heard of the Man in the Moon? Many people say they can see a man's face on the Moon's surface. Others see a rabbit. What do you see?

What Makes the Moon Shine?

The Moon is the brightest object in the night sky. The Moon does not make its own light. Light from the Sun **reflects**, or bounces off, the Moon's surface. Without the Sun's light, we would not be able to see the Moon from Earth.

The Moon reflects the Sun's light the way the mirror reflects the light from the flashlight in the activity on the next page. Neither the mirror nor the Moon makes its own light. They both reflect light.

Like the Moon, the planets in the solar system also reflect the Sun's light.

ACTIVITY: Reflecting the Moon

What You Will Need

- a flashlight
- a mirror
- Styrofoam ball
- two friends

Steps

Step 1: One person holds the flashlight—the Sun. One person holds the mirror—the Moon. The last person holds the ball—Earth.

Step 2: All three people stand to form a triangle.

Step 3: Turn off the lights. Can you see the ball?

Step 4: Turn on the flashlight. Shine the flashlight into the mirror.

Step 5: Hold the mirror so the light reflects onto the ball. Can you see the ball? You have just demonstrated how the Moon reflects light onto Earth.

Safety Rule

Do not shine the flashlight into your own or anyone else's eyes. It can harm them.

The Moon in Motion

The Moon and planets are always moving! The planets orbit the Sun. The Moon orbits Earth. It takes about 28 days for the Moon to orbit, or travel once around Earth.

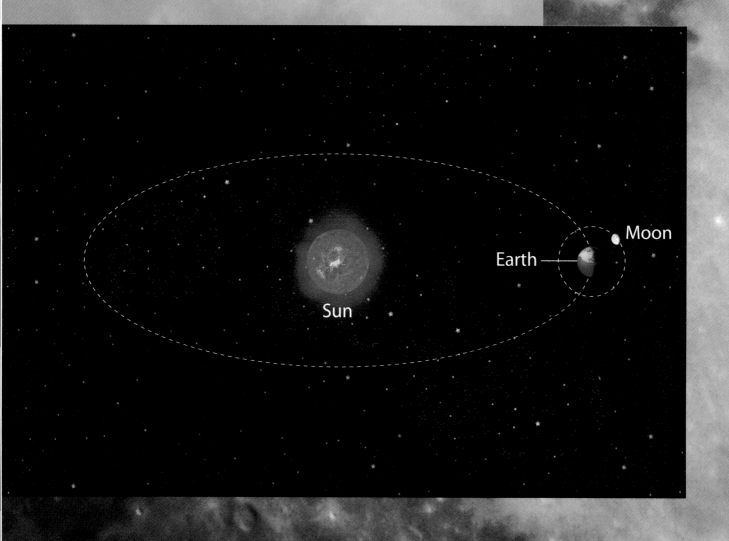

Sun

Earth

Moon

The Moon also **rotates**, or spins, as it orbits Earth. The Moon rotates on its **axis**. The axis is an imaginary line through the middle of the Moon from its top to its bottom. It takes the Moon about 28 days to make one complete rotation on its axis. It takes the Moon about the same amount of time to orbit once around Earth. This means that the same side of the Moon always faces Earth.

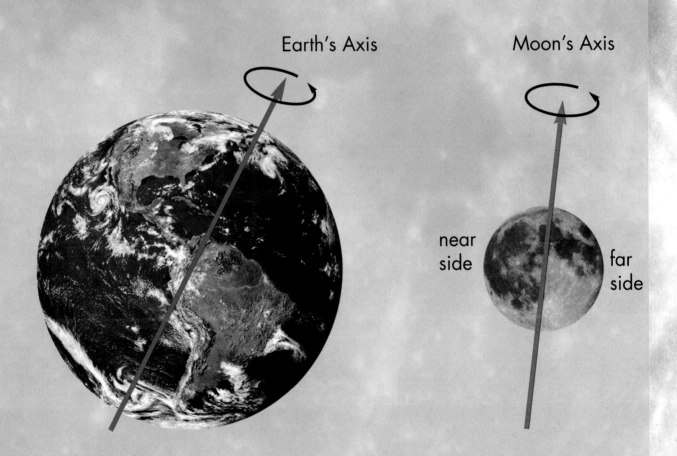

Earth's Axis

Moon's Axis

near side

far side

Earth and the Moon each rotate on an axis. The side of the Moon that faces Earth is called the near side. The side of the Moon that is always turned away from Earth is called the far side.

Changing Shape

Have you ever noticed that the Moon appears to change shape each night? This is because we can only see the part of the Moon that is lit by the Sun. As the Moon orbits Earth, the Sun's light shines on different amounts of the Moon's surface. The shape of the lit part of the Moon is called a **phase**. The Moon has eight phases. The phases follow a **pattern**. It takes about four weeks to complete the pattern. Learn more about the Moon's phases on pages 16 and 17.

The Moon's shape and size appear to change with each phase.

Phases of the Moon

The first phase is called the new moon. We cannot see the Moon during the new moon phase. This is because the Moon is between the Sun and Earth. In this position, light reflects only off the side of the Moon we cannot see.

The waxing crescent comes after the new moon. The word "waxing" is used to describe the Moon when more of the Moon is visible each night.

Start a Moon diary! Draw a picture of the Moon each day for 28 days. You will be able to see the Moon's phases in action.

The next three phases of the Moon are the first quarter, waxing gibbous, and full moon. During a full moon the Sun lights the entire side of the Moon facing Earth.

After the Moon becomes full, it starts waning. The word "waning" is used to describe the Moon when less of the Moon is visible each night. The last three phases are the waning gibbous, last quarter, and waning crescent. Then, the phases start over again.

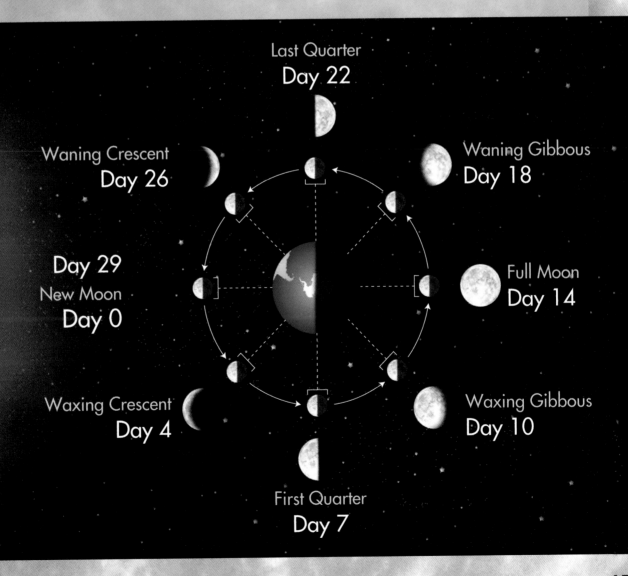

Last Quarter
Day 22

Waning Crescent
Day 26

Waning Gibbous
Day 18

Day 29
New Moon
Day 0

Full Moon
Day 14

Waxing Crescent
Day 4

Waxing Gibbous
Day 10

First Quarter
Day 7

Lunar Eclipse

A lunar **eclipse** takes place when the Moon is full and passes through Earth's shadow. This causes Earth to block all or part of the Sun's light from reaching the Moon. Small amounts of sunlight are able to reach the Moon. The light that reaches the Moon can be deep red or orange. This can give the Moon a red glow. A lunar eclipse may occur two to four times a year, only during a full moon. These eclipses can only be seen at night.

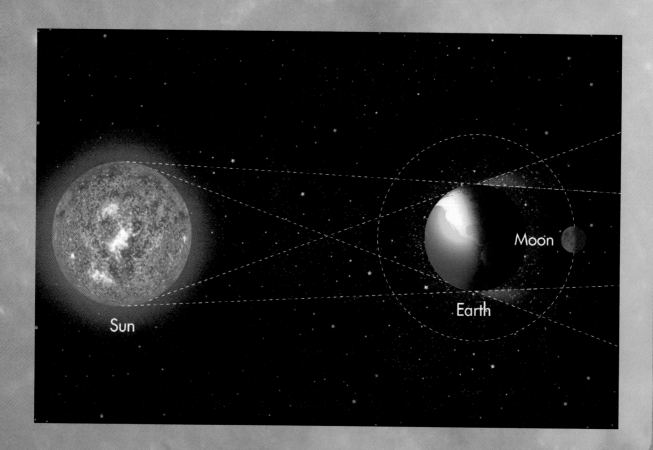

Sun

Moon

Earth

During a lunar eclipse, it can take the Moon more than an hour to completely pass through Earth's shadow.

Mission to the Moon!

Other than Earth, the Moon is the only place in our solar system humans have visited. On July 20, 1969, **astronauts** Neil Armstrong and Edwin "Buzz" Aldrin landed the Lunar Module, a vehicle that was part of their Apollo 11 spacecraft, on the Moon's surface. Neil Armstrong was the first person to set foot on the Moon. His famous words after his first step were

This bootprint marks one of the first steps humans took on the Moon.

"That's one small step for man—one giant leap for mankind."

What do you think Armstrong meant? Would you like to visit the Moon someday? Maybe you will follow in his famous footsteps!

The Moon Rocks!

Astronauts collected samples of rocks and soil from the Moon. These samples have helped us learn more about the Moon.

Learning More

WEBSITES

www.nasakids.com

Visit NASA Kids' Club for challenging space games and to learn about the latest information about space.

http://starchild.gsfc.nasa.gov/docs/StarChild/StarChild.html

StarChild is a learning center for young astronomers created by NASA. This website offers exciting images and activities.

www.kidsastronomy.com/astroskymap/lunar.htm

Find information about the current and upcoming Moon phases.

www.childrensuniversity.manchester.ac.uk/interactives/ science/earthandbeyond/phases.asp

This website shows how the positions of the Sun and Earth affect our view of the Moon.

OTHER BOOKS IN THIS SERIES

The Stars

The Planets

The Sun

Glossary

astronauts (AS-truh-nawtz) People trained to travel and work in space

axis (AK-sihs) An imaginary straight line around which an object spins

craters (KRAY-turz) Holes caused by objects hitting the surface of a planet or moon

eclipse (ih-KLIHPS) When one space object partly or completely hides another space object

orbits (OR-bitz) Travels around another object in a single path in space

pattern A set of events that is repeated

phase (FAYZ) A step or stage in a number of events that happen over and over

plains Large areas of flat land

reflects (rih-FLEHKTS) Bounces waves of light back from a surface

rotates Turns about a center point or an axis

spheres Ball-shaped objects

Index